Music Minus One

BASSOON

Includes Demonstration and Backing Tracks Online

SOLOS *for the* BASSOON PLAYER

T0081479

PLAYBACK+
Speed • Pitch • Balance • Loop

To access audio visit:
www.halleonard.com/mylibrary

2851-1212-5809-4788

ISBN 978-1-59615-646-3

Music Minus One

EXCLUSIVELY DISTRIBUTED BY

HAL•LEONARD®

© 1996 MMO Music Group, Inc.
All Rights Reserved

For all works contained herein:
Unauthorized copying, arranging, adapting, recording, Internet posting, public performance,
or other distribution of the printed or recorded music in this publication is an infringement of copyright.
Infringers are liable under the law.

Visit Hal Leonard Online at
www.halleonard.com

CONTENTS

Bourrée I and II

Third Cello Suite

2 taps (2 meas.) precede bassoon
Piano enters on 3rd bassoon note.

Poco allegro

Johann Sebastian Bach (1685-1750)

I

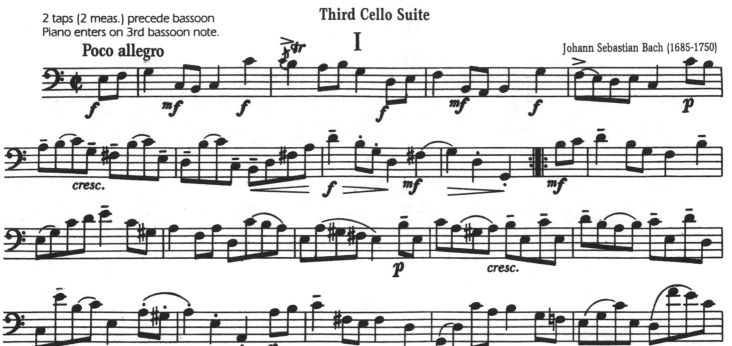

II

D. C. Bourrée I

Es ist vollbracht
(It is finished)

from: St. John Passion

4 taps (1 meas.) precede piano on downbeat.

Molto Adagio

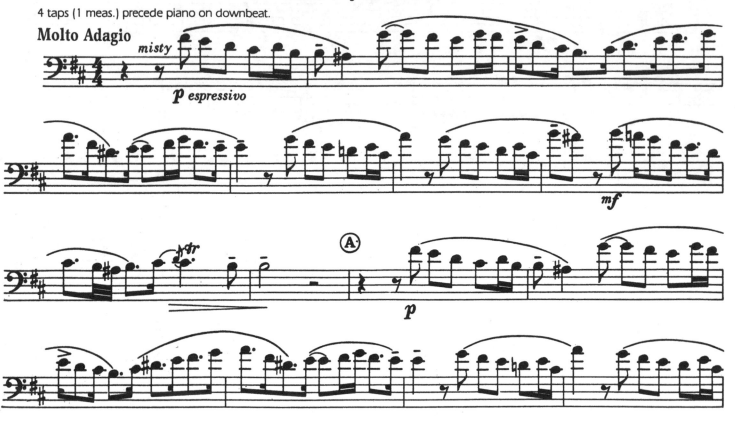

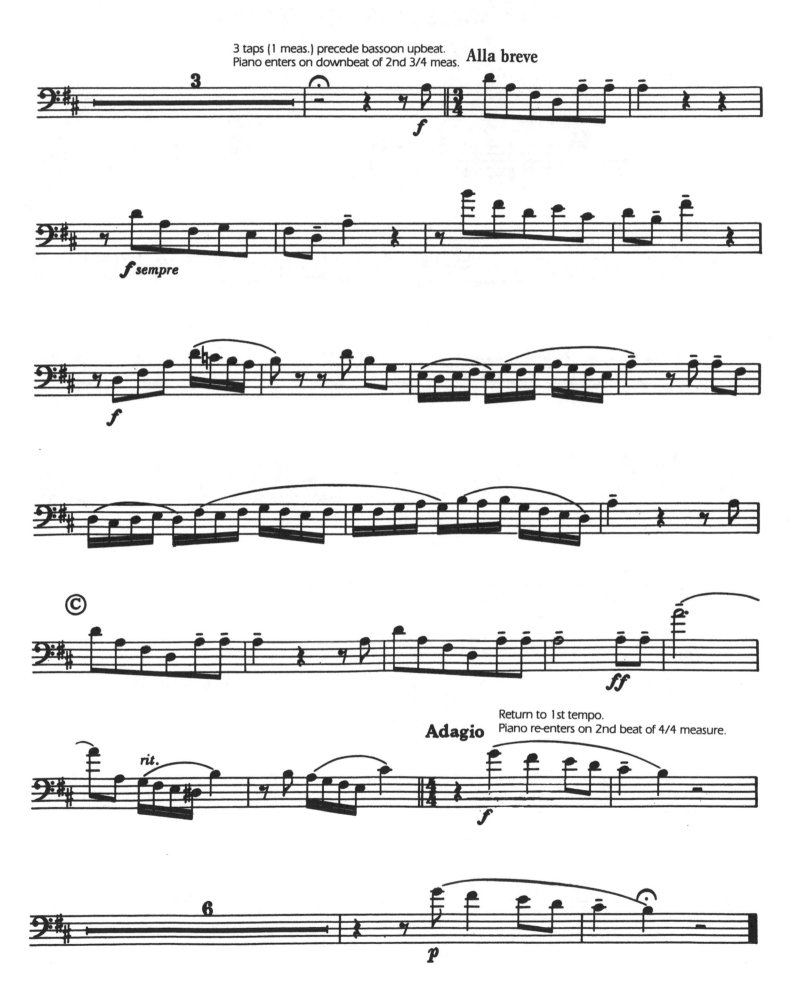

5

The Sorcerer's Apprentice
(L'apprenti sorcier)

Paul Dukas (1865-1935)

Berceuse

from: The Firebird

Igor Stravinsky (1882-1971)

Entra'acte

Carmen

George Bizet (1838-1975)

4 taps (2 meas.) precede bassoon
and piano entrance.

Allegro moderato

Adagio

from Sexter, Op. 71

Ludwig van Beethoven (1770-1827)

4 taps (2 meas.) precede bassoon and piano entrance.

Romanza
(Una furtiva lagrima)

from: L'elisir d'amore

Gaetano Donizetti (1797-1848)

6 taps (1 meas.) precede piano entrance
on downbeat of 1st measure.

Larghetto

Pictures at an Exhibition
(Four excerpts)

I Promenade

5 taps (1 meas.) precede bassoon entrance
on downbeat of 1st measure. Piano enters
on 3rd measure and re-enters on downbeat 7th measure.

Moderato commodo assai e con delicatezza

Modest Mussorgsky (1839-1881)

Attacca II

2 taps (1 meas.) precede piano and bassoon entrance. **II The Old Castle**
Piano plays again on 4th 8th beat of 2nd measure.

Andante molto cantabile e con dolore ♩.= 60

14

III Promenade

Piano Solo **Moderato non tanto, pesantemente**

2 taps (1 meas.) precede piano on downbeat of 1st measure **IV Ox-cart**

Sempre moderato pesante

First Movement

Symphony No. 4 in F Minor

3 taps (1 meas.) precede piano and bassoon entrance

Andante sostenuto

Peter I. Tschaikowsky, Op. 36

Moderato con anima 3 taps (1 meas.) precede bassoon entrance after 3rd tap.
Piano enters on 3rd bassoon note.

Meno mosso Piano re-enters on 2nd beat.

Moderato assai quasi andante

Moderato assai quasi andante

Second Movement

Symphony No. 4 in F Minor

3 taps (1½ meas.) precede bassoon entrance on the
And of 1st beat.

Andantino in modo di canzona

Peter I. Tschaikowsky

p cantabile

mf

Piano plays on downbeats of measures.
At Tempo 1 piano plays on downbeat of this measure
and on downbeat of 2nd measure.

Più mosso

mf

f

rit.

Tempo I

pp

espress.

pp

pp

morendo

Valse
(Third movement)
Symphony No. 5 in E Minor

Peter I. Tschaikowsky, Op. 64
(1840-1893)
Arranged by S.S.

3 taps (1 meas.) precede piano entrance on downbeat of
1st measure.

Allegro moderato ♩ = 138

21

JANET GRICE

Janet Grice is a musician versed in jazz, classical, and Brazilian music. She draws upon her varied musical background in her work as a performer and teacher. She has played bassoon with leading composers of both jazz and new music, touring and recording in the USA, Brazil, and Europe. Chamber music appearances include the Carnegie Recital Hall and Kennedy Center, and with her own ensembles in libraries and museums. Her Brazilian Jazz group performed in concerts and clubs internationally, including the Lake George Jazz Festival, Dampzentrale in Switzerland, and the American Consulate in Brazil. A recipient of numerous grants from the National Endowment for the Arts for jazz study and performance, she has composed and arranged music for jazz ensembles, producing two CDs of her music. "Song for Andy" was recorded in Brazil, and "The Muse" in New York. Both feature Janet's bassoon and recorder playing. As a Fullbright Fellow, Janet spent a year researching Brazilian instrumental music. She has visited Brazil many times and speaks fluent Portuguese. Janet freelances in New York and is a member of the Crosstown Ensemble, an orchestra for new music. As a teacher, Janet has extensive classroom experience at all levels, and has been a private teacher of bassoon, recorder, guitar, and clarinet. She has taught jazz improvisation and led student ensembles while a graduate assistant at New York University, and has taught professional educators in courses at the Lincoln Center Institute and Arts Exel Institute. At present Janet is a teaching artist for the Lincoln Center Institute, Carnegie Hall "Link-Up" program, and the Westchester Arts Council. She is director of the Westchester Symphony's Young People's Music Workshops and a music auditor for the New York State Council on the Arts. Janet leads music workshops for children that focus on multi-cultural musical experiences, improvisation, and composition. She encourages collaboration and creativity, helping children explore and discover music through hands-on activities.

Janet received a Bachelor of Music degree in Bassoon Performance from New England Conservatory of Music and a Master of Music degree in Jazz Composition from New York University. Her teachers have included Ran Blake, Jim McNeely, Stephen Maxym, and George Coleman. In addition to her musical activities, Janet is the mother of two young boys.

HARRIET WINGREEN

Harriet Wingreen, a native New Yorker, studied on fellowship at the Juilliard Graduate School. As a member of the New York Chamber Soloists and the Lyric Trio, Ms. Wingreen toured extensively as a chamber music performer in the United States, Europe, the Soviet Union, Canada, Mexico, South America, and the Far East, and has performed with many leading singers and instrumentalists. In addition to her position as a pianist and celeste player with the New York Philharmonic, she assists the conductors and soloists in the preparation of their performances with the orchestra. She also performs frequently in the New York Philharmonic Ensembles chamber music concerts at Merkin Concert Hall and Rockefeller University. Ms. Wingreen is on the faculty of the Manhattan School of Music, where she teaches in the orchestral instruments Masters Degree program. She has recorded for Monitor, Vanguard, Decca, Lyrichord, CRI, Golden Crest, Classic Editions, Cambria, and New World Records.

MORE GREAT CLARINET PUBLICATIONS FROM

Music Minus One

CLASSICAL PUBLICATIONS

Advanced Contest Solos for Clarinet, Volume 1
Brahms • Hindemith • Mozart
Performed by Stanley Drucker
Accompaniment: Judith Olson, piano
Book/Online Audio
00400630............................$14.99

Also available:
Advanced Clarinet Solos, Volume 2
00400321 Book/Online Audio $14.99
Advanced Clarinet Solos, Volume 4
00400322 Book/CD Pack......................................$14.99

Johannes Brahms – Clarinet Quintet in B Minor, Op. 115
Performed by Collete Galante
Accompaniment: The Classic String Quartet
Book/Online Audio
00400323 ....$19.99

Johannes Brahms – Sonatas for Clarinet and Piano, Op. 120
No. 1 in F Minor & No. 2 in E-Flat Minor
Performed by Jerome Bunke
Accompaniment: Hidemitsu Hayashi, piano
Book/2-CD Set
00400046......................$19.99

The Clarinetist
Classical Pieces for Clarinet and Piano
Performed by Anton Hollich
Accompaniment: Harriet Wingreen, piano
Book/2-CD Set
00400122 ....$14.99

Clarinet Solos
Weber – Concertino, Op. 26 & Beethoven – Trio No. 4, Op. 11
Performed by Keith Dwyer
Accompaniment: The Stuttgart Festival Orchestra
Book/Online Audio
00400605.......................$19.99

W.A. Mozart – Clarinet Concerto in A Major, KV 622

Performed by Denitza Lavchieva
Accompaniment: Tempi Concertati Chamber Orchestra
Book/Online Audio
00400047 ....$19.99

W.A. Mozart – Quintet for Clarinet and Strings in A Major, KV581 "Stadler"

Performed by Keith Dwyer
Accompaniment: The Cassini Ensemble
Book/Online Audio
00400314.........................$19.99

Robert Schumann – Fantasy Pieces, Op. 73 & Three Romances, Op. 94

Performed by Jerome Bunke
Accompaniment: Hidemitsu Hayashi, piano
Book/Online Audio
00400316......................$14.99

Carl Maria von Weber – Clarinet Concerto No. 1 F Minor, Op. 73 & Carl Stamitz – Concerto No. 3 in B-Flat Major
Performed by Keith Dwyer
Accompaniment: Stuttgart Festival Orchestra
Book/Online Audio
00400586......................$19.99

POP/STANDARDS

Play the Music of Burt Bacharach

Performed by Tim Gordon
Accompaniment: The Jack Six All-Star Orchestra
Book/CD Pack
00400636 ....$14.99

Sinatra Set to Music
Performed by Ron Odrich
Accompaniment: The Al Raymond Orchestra
Book/Online Audio
00400711.......................$14.99

JAZZ/SWING

From Dixie to Swing
For Clarinet & Soprano Sax
Performed by Kenny Davern
Accompaniment: The Dick Wellstood All-Stars
Book/Online Audio
00400613...........................$14.99

New Orleans Classics
Performed by Tim Laughlin
Accompaniment: Tim Laughlin's New Orleans All Stars
Book/Online Audio
00400024 ....$19.99

Swing with a Band

Performed by Tim Gordon
Book/Online Audio
00400637 ....$14.99

What Is This Thing Called Jazz?
A Jazz Man's Approach to Great Standards
Performed by Ron Odrich
Book/CD Pack
00400681 ....$14.99

To see a full listing of
Music Minus One publications, visit
halleonard.com/MusicMinusOne

Music Minus One

HAL•LEONARD®
Prices, contents, and availability subject
to change without notice.

MORE GREAT SAXOPHONE PUBLICATIONS FROM

Music Minus One

ADVANCED ALTO SAX SOLOS – VOLUME 1
Performed by Paul Brodie, alto saxophone
Accompaniment: Antonin Kubalek, piano

Virtuoso Paul Brodie introduces you to the world of advanced alto sax solos with this wide-ranging collection. Contains performance suggestions and Mr. Brodie's incredible interpretations to help you achieve greatness! Includes a printed music score containing the solo part, annotated with performance suggestions; and access to professional recordings with complete versions (with soloist) followed by piano accompaniments to each piece, minus the soloist. Includes works by Vivaldi, Jacob, Whitney, and Benson.

00400602 Book/Online Audio..............................**$16.99**

ADVANCED ALTO SAX SOLOS – VOLUME 2
Performed by Vincent Abato, alto saxophone
Accompaniment: Harriet Wingreen, piano

Listen as extraordinary virtuoso Vincent Abato of the Metropolitan Opera Orchestra takes you further into the advanced repertoire with these spectacular sax selections. Listen to his masterful interpretations, examine his performance suggestions, then you step in and make magic with Harriet Wingreen, legendary piano accompanist for the New York Philharmonic. Includes: Schubert "The Bee," Rabaud "Solo de Concours," and Creston "Sonata, Op. 19" 2nd and 3rd movements. Includes a printed music score containing the solo part, annotated with performance suggestions; and tracks with complete versions (with soloist) followed by piano accompaniments to each piece, minus the soloist.

00400603 Book/Online Audio..............................**$16.99**

PLAY THE MUSIC OF BURT BACHARACH
ALTO OR TENOR SAXOPHONE

Along with lyricist Hal David, Burt Bacharach penned some of the best pop songs and standards of all time. These superb collections let solo instrumentalists play along with: Alfie • Blue on Blue • Do You Know the Way to San Jose • I Say a Little Prayer • Magic Moments • This Guy's in Love with You • Walk on By • What the World Needs Now • The Windows of the World • and Wives and Lovers.

00400657 Book/Online Audio..............................**$22.99**

BOSSA, BONFÁ & BLACK ORPHEUS FOR TENOR SAXOPHONE – A TRIBUTE TO STAN GETZ
TENOR SAXOPHONE
featuring Glenn Zottola

Original transcriptions for you to perform! The bossa novas that swept the world in 1950 created a whole new set of songs to equal the great standards of the '20s, '30s and '40s by Gershwin, Porter, Arlen, Berlin, Kern and Rodgers. This collection for tenor sax is a tribute to the great Stan Getz and includes: Black Orpheus • Girl from Ipanema • Gentle Rain • One Note Samba • Once I Loved • Dindi • Baubles, Bangles and Beads • Meditation • Triste • I Concentrate on You • Samba de Orfeu.

00124387 Book/Online Audio..............................**$16.99**

CLASSIC STANDARDS FOR ALTO SAXOPHONE
A TRIBUTE TO JOHNNY HODGES
featuring Bob Wilber

Ten classic standards are presented in this book as they were arranged for the Neal Heft String Orchestra in 1954, including: Yesterdays • Laura • What's New? • Blue Moon • Can't Help Lovin' Dat Man • Embraceable You • Willow Weep for Me • Memories of You • Smoke Gets in Your Eyes • Stardust. Bob Wilber performs the songs on the provided CD on soprano saxophone, although they are translated for alto saxophone.

00131389 Book/Online Audio..............................**$16.99**

EASY JAZZ DUETS FOR 2 ALTO SAXOPHONES AND RHYTHM SECTION
Performed by Hal McKusick, alto saxophone
Accompaniment: The Benny Goodman Rhythm Section: George Duvivier, bass; Bobby Donaldson, drums

This great collection of jazz duets gives you the opportunity to accompany saxophonist Hal McKusick and the Benny Goodman Rhythm Section. Suitable for beginning players, all the selections are great fun. This album allows you to play either duet part. Includes printed musical score with access to online audio tracks: you hear both parts played in stereo, then each duet is repeated with the first part omitted and then the second part, so you can play along.

00400480 Book/Online Audio..............................**$16.99**

FROM DIXIE TO SWING
CLARINET OR SOPRANO SAX
Performed by Kenny Davern, clarinet
Accompaniment: Kenny Davern, clarinet & soprano sax; 'Doc' Cheatham, trumpet; Vic Dickenson, trombone; Dick Wellstood, piano; George Duvivier, bass; Gus Johnson Jr., drums

Such jazz legends as Dick Wellstood, Alphonse 'Doc' Cheatham and George Duvivier and more back you up in this amazing collection of New York-style Dixieland standards. After the break-up of the big-band era around 1950, many of the finest 'swing' or mainstream players found themselves without an outlet for their abilities and took to playing 'Dixieland' in New York clubs such as Eddie Condon's and the Metropole. And so was born a new style of Dixieland jazz minus the banjos, tubas, steamboats and magnolias! It is this version we celebrate on this album. We encourage you, the soloist, to invent counter-melodies rather than mere harmony parts. This is a music of loose weaving parts, not one of precision ensemble figures. And in short, it is one of the greatest improvisational experiences any jazz player could hope to have. Includes a printed music score and online audio access to stereo accompaniments to each piece.

00400613 Book/Online Audio..............................**$16.99**

GLAZUNOV – CONCERTO IN E-FLAT MAJOR, OP. 109; VON KOCH – CONCERTO IN E-FLAT MAJOR
ALTO SAXOPHONE
Performed by Lawrence Gwozdz, alto saxophone
Accompaniment: Plovdiv Philharmonic Orchestra
Conductor: Nayden Todorov

Alexander Glazunov, one of the great masters of late Russian Romanticism, was fascinated by the saxophone and by jazz. In 1934 he wrote this beautiful saxophone concerto which has become a classic, combining romanticism with modern idioms as well. Erland von Koch's 1958 saxophone concerto is filled with experimental modern tonalities and fantastic effects for the saxophone. Both are must-haves for the serious saxophonist. Includes a printed music score; informative liner notes; and online audio featuring the concerti performed twice: first with soloist, then again with orchestral accompaniment only, minus you, the soloist. The audio is accessed online using the unique code inside each book and can be streamed or downloaded.

00400487 Book/Online Audio..............................**$16.99**

To see a full listing of Music Minus One publications, visit
www.halleonard.com/MusicMinusOne

Prices, contents, and availability subject to change without notice.